Amazin' Transcendence

A Book of Poetry and Opinionated Writing

By: Jeremy Adams

Contents

Part 3: Love

Part 4: Perspective

Part 7: Metamorphosis Changing Identity

Epilogue

Acknowledgements

I WILL CHANGE THE WORLD.

Every morning I wake up, and I tell myself that it is a day that I will change the world positively. I do not see the world as a bad place, but there are many things that can change. I do believe one single person has the power to change and I understand that there are trillions of other people in the world that are not satisfied with their circumstances. I have not lost faith in humanity to live better, but I want to change the world because I feel a passion to fight for positivity, and enlightenment.

The problem with society is that we have become blind to the issues that really matter. Unknowingly, we have lost our own humanity within our own cultural systems. I do not need to be president of the United States when I grow up. I do not desire to be the richest man alive . I want to be a man of faith, and change. A man who looks back on his soul to recall the number of notable things he did for his people. I want to stand for a purpose, and feel excited for the things that matter.

I refuse to be a crook, manipulator, trader, sellout, and a fool like the people we call social leaders today. I refuse to think inside the box to be influenced by propaganda. I do not need to be a leader of any company or organization to think for me. I do not want to control peoples' thoughts. I want to be myself, and I want to help people gain perspective. I want to make people think critically about the world they live in.

I am on a mission for greatness to expand on my gifts. I cannot fail because I won't accept failure as an option. I will continue the legacy of every person that ever led their people in the right path against the corrupt powers that fought even harder to make the world worst. Even though their lives most likely ended in tragedies, they will live on forever as men and women who stood for a cause greater than themselves. I will never accept propaganda when I know the truth is in within me.

This book is for the people that say that one single person cannot change the world. The legacy starts from as high as the president all the way down to a 22 year old that attends a Deaf university in DC with no name. I truly believe all it takes is one person to begin to change the mindset of those around them through truth, compassion, and loyalty. All it takes is that one person who is not afraid to defy the odds, and become the social leader that people have been missing since the times of feminism, and civil rights. We should not be afraid to change the world because the world is so ready for change.

To live as a mere mortal is a blessing bestowed upon us, but to have the choice of truth is the curse that haunts our thoughts. Chaos looms, and hearts are filled with sorrows while the brains are filled with lies to keep our minds in chains of slavery. The time is now where we free minds, and take back what is rightfully ours. We must free ourselves from slavery of mind, and enlighten ourselves to keep it.

Part 1: FEAR

Dilemma

Fear and shame is the reason why people do not achieve their potential. Fear is the reason why people do not feel themselves worthy of greatness. Fear is the reason why people live as if they are dead already. We fear that we will fail or fall short and that shame then has the power to keep a person dead inside. You will never transcend those limits where your dreams await if you do not realize that anything is possible. There is a part of me that wants to write for the people, and be that voice that enriches the lives of others. I started writing because it made me feel that I was making a difference to a world of injustice. I thought that people would see my soul pour out onto each and every page.

My dilemma is that I want to write to help others, but I feel that people do not read. I feel I am writing for personal gain. I was always fine with the fact that even my parents never read the things I wrote, but one day this dilemma became apparent to me when I was watching this video from awarforoursouls.com. I watched the video, and it was utterly sickening to see that this guy had become so popular for a video about issues I have been writing about as a black youth (the age group that he has trying to reach). I was sickened by the fact that millions of people of all ages had watched this video and were so emotionally compelled to his assumed ignorance of black youth. Black youth may be perceived as ignorant, and rebellious because of these videos but when the youth actually try to change something they are sidelined or un-noticed because they are too young. I told my dad about how terrible the video was because I had been writing about these things for months, but he said "whatever". That was the first time I experienced my writers dilemma.

Fear Itself

Fear is the presence of the unconscious

Brain resonating the nerves that control
your every move

But fear does not resonate truth

The proof is in the fate of things not seen

And they are not seen because fear
overcame those particular dreams

It seems that fear grows in the identity we
never knew we had

But that mean green comes out of us
avenging its denial

Our fear is the phoenix that drives us crazy

But it's that very fear of our dreams that
makes us realize everything

Tired

That can't stand, cant move type of feeling

When your feet are glued to your mood,
and on the insole of your shoes type of
feeling

Your heart pumps there in the balance

Weighted solely on the person you
expected to stand there strongly

That sick feeling when you can feel your
insides peeling back

Your lack of restraint tells you to hit the
wall as hard as you can

Because the man standing before you
stands in love

Out of the graces of fate you have found
someone

But that someone has found something
greater that leaves you nothing but Tired

Disconnection

Have you ever disconnected your senses?

Left on the fence between living, and barely existing

I have gone backwards in my thinking that I was actually thinkin

The being within me nearly hangs from the tree of knowledge

Hoping that it will fix me

Hoping that it will teach me to be me

Though I am lost, who isn't?

Even once you find yourself you can still forget it

Becoming a stranger to the imperfections you once understood

Unable to see under the life you came from to the life you have become

Because the changes coming

Suicide

This poem was made for reading

Heart being out of your chest

Mind racing, fingers pacing across my QWERTY telling a story for Glory

Not only for me but for all powers intended to make you sour

I will devour myself before I devour mankind's crucible for Love

Speaker of the truth assassinated and irritated mentally

I will not cooperate with corporations or the orientation process of the job I applied for when I was born

Coexist to this poem relinquishing self

Look into the hole in your soul that needs filling and that's exactly where this poem goes

Looking

Sometimes I find myself looking

But the predicate of the matter seems as though does not matter

Stress racing through my body-heart beating fast as my muscles contract

Another victim of the minds powers

Built to devour anything formed against it

Running from myself I am more afraid of things to come

Becoming the one is even less likely than becoming a bum in this Matrix

Impossible to escape these feeling I keep running from this Matrix to the serenity where the pad meets the pen

Then I realize in order to win I have to stop running

I am defeating myself in the same breath, ultimately killing two birds with one stone

Part 2:
DREAMS

Be Yourself

What is "be yourself"? The words have become a cliché, but we can look around and notice there are people that have accepted who they are, and those who strive to be someone else. The term is mistaken to mean be as twisted as possible to show people individuality. It is mistaken to mean imitating how others act to fit in, but I feel that the true meaning of "be yourself" is to accept yourself for who you are. It means to come to the realization that no one will ever be fully accepted in this world, and realize that it is up to you whether you can deal with that. People cannot be afraid to explore new worlds and ideas that interest them because another person thinks they're lame or weird. Individuality can help you understand that being yourself means to extend the social norms and put your own stamp no matter what your social class may be. We are all valuable to this world in some way. Other genuine people will always accept genuine people, but the first step to change is finding the courage to examine your own life. This can be a lifelong process, but it could even save your life. My dreams are to one day be as original to myself without trying to live up to others expectations. My dreams are to transcend the materialistic values of capitalist society, and truly live for peace.

Dreamer

I can listen to the poet speak all day long

But what is wrong is the dreamer can't sit
in this world

So your mother tells you to come in

Afraid you'll become one of those hippie
kids

She disses it

The one thing you love,

Says its bullshit and her goal for you is to
get rich

That's when the rebel and his henchman
get that twitch

That Lilo and Stitch

Me want honeycombs shit

Even though I respect you to the utmost
that upmost has its boundaries

I know family is god chosen

But to boast in the frozen heart of those that have been woven into your subconscious does not fit me

I have pity for those not dreaming

And if that means the thing thicker than water is faultier than a drip of water then I falter

I will not stop dreaming because the family tells me that it means nothing

It's just too bad

I thought we had something!

Thank You

I will never know what it is like to be a
being oppressed by his own history

Caught within the chains that look to
comfort me

I reject the devils ignorance

Bathed in deliverance I see what we have
really come to be

Tired of fighting the system we become the
system

For those who continue to lead they run
from the system

Only to find those strong enough to fight
back

The cave is harder to come out of when the
means for going within has changed

Never understanding the Matrix within
ourselves

I only dream to humble myself in its virtues

Poetry

You don't just wake up one day and
become a poet

Like greatness you don't even realize you
show it

Poetry grows inside of you like truth does

Mingles within the sands of time as proof
does to come out squeaky clean

Living your own dreams under immoral
means only leads to one thing

More money more problems

While the rest of us sit high on our
realization of enlightening

You metaphor on the floor next to your
weakness screaming lies to the weakest

Without using like or as you bypass each
truth that defines your existence

As the persistence on this road stares off at
a distance

Gasping

They say integrity is who you are when no one is watching

I'm by myself right now so….

 I guess the crowd will only see my words

My redemption song as I look to Zion

Attempting to battle this python with his greedy hands on everything I see

My soul lies within these poems

Spilled out my heart to simply receive

"I like that, when did you write that?"

Afraid that no one will ever see my inner me he lies on a Tumblr page for everyone to peek

Step right up, and take a gander at the circus on a page

Guaranteed to leave you insane

Powerful enough to question the sane

Seems people only pay attention when you're living the dream

Swear they were a part of your team and are always asking for something

Meanwhile they weren't there while you were dying trying to manipulate reality

I am gasping writing these poems for the ghost that don't take notice

It will be Okay

It will be okay little Black Girl

Mother Nature will come for you, and comfort you so don't give up

You are the essence of man dipped in turmoil and sold off as weak creatures

But your strength is within you and resonates from inevitability

You are an endless drive pushed inside the sands of time

Your beauty isn't measurable to what size heel you get or the size of your hips and breast

You are the gatekeeper his world is much more priceless to all our answers and half the solution

 It is impossible to understand a man but limitless to understand the wisdom of you little black girl

This Is

This is Shakur at his best

This is a genius to a test

This is better sarcasm and jokes puff toked
pass the inhalation of man

This is *a Legends of the Fall*

No speech only the movement of words
fixed so eloquent across the paper

This residue will vapor into the moon only
no to be seen

Even though it seems not to be there it is

Same as the being you see before you

Designed through opinion but defined by
truth

Afraid of all the stressing you pull back on
the bottle and pull the trigger

The blast leaves the figure of your very soul
in pieces afraid to be the leaser

You allow people to take your brain and give you a name

Tobey, Tom, Tim and all the other cabins we inevitably put ourselves in

But choose not to come out

This poem isn't controversial but is about black people

Reduced to mere nothingness on a wall of shame in this game were playing

Don't you want better?

Don't you want your children to know Election Day instead of possession day?

Don't give away your dream and trade it for your perception of real

Don't be someone that you're not 'cuz the plot only thickens and the less righteous are first for the devils picking

Elevation

Mind Elevation is our reason

The treason is you haven't even touched the surface of your own mind

Meaning that your findings are still slowly winding downward

Metaphoric for the ignorance you portray keeps conscious mind elevation away

Leaving the real liberators afraid to lead his people

The true hope can't be seen because we're living in a dream world

Where little boys and girls are rocking each other's worlds and grown men are joining in on the party

Where our political parties are the prosecutor of their own crime

Ironically the defendant is the working class

The glass of time doesn't exist

Each and every person thinks that their only way out is one simple slit of the wrist

Vertical that is, 'cuz that's the only way to get that true kick

Any other way and you're faced with knowing you couldn't go through it

You know you truly didn't want to do it

Now your depressive state and your means for living have become congruent

Tangent to the being of man

Your true nature and your creator are at a standoff in that downward spiral

Lost in the self trial

The dial becomes a little bit easier to turn

But the lock is still unable to open because the pass code is unknown

What You Don't See

It's crazy how those with the least are those with the most

How a man that is blind sees more than the dark screen you envision

How a woman that is deaf hears louder than submission

How a man with no legs can run a 5k race

How a woman with no arms can lift the heaviest of weights

But what you can't imagine is the heart these individuals have

How they can just sit back and look on their life, and laugh

But all we see is our struggles that haunt our past

So next time you think you can't do it

Think about the people that live their lives every day to prove it

What are your Dreams made of?

I have written 11 thousand words in 66 poems

But my true dream is to put down the pen and show them

Give them away like Turkey's on Christmas Day

I know it sounds cliché, but the writer in me is only pleased by one thing

Reading

I want to look back and say that I accomplished something

Not famous for running away from my ambitions

So I run toward them

Hoping that one day I will pick up speed

Those are the things that my dreams are made of

Transcending

I want to transcend as far as my dreams
will carry

The fairytale feeling that we can actually be
what we dream

Found only in caves where the enlightened
have crawled out

I want greatness without backlash

No crash later because of past decisions

I need that intangible

End of the game and I'm the blame for the
win

Twin to failure, winning is the sweeter of
the two

But not long lasting nor guaranteed

You preserve those moral victories

Part 3: LOVE

What is Love?

People make love seem like it is rocket science because they feel that it is a complicated matter. When we meditate on love it becomes a basic concept. It is best to watch children, and their love for their parent to understand the true nature of love. We can watch couples that have been married for thirty years to understand the true nature of love. Love can be Platonic. Sometimes love can be mistaken to be lust, but it is more than the feeling of stimulation for 15 to 30 minutes. Love will make people do crazy things, but it always seems worth it. Love will make you sacrifice things you want for the things others may need. Love is everything it is thought it to be because it has no wrong answer, just a difference in perspective.

The Game

The game of Love is a game of winners and losers that we all play. It is full of walls, and conquerors. It is a game of cycles. It is a game of emotions. It is a game that will trap someone so deep that they can lose their ability to feel anything at all. It is a game of building, and taking all your money out right before that everything crashes. It is a game of averages and odds. It is a game of search and destroy. The "Cycle" our games create is inevitable to encounter. It is designed for people looking to be in a relationship either because they cannot stand being lonely or they feel they need a relationship to be happy. They don't realize that being in a relationship is sometimes nothing more than a social stigma. The key to breaking the cycle of this game is self worth. There are too many people that form a need to be loved without even finding love from within their self. The results are women that do not realize their worth, and men who cannot trust a woman. The truth is that we cannot play games when it comes to love. The game has turned generations of people into bitter and hopeless romantics that bash Love.

When people realize that playing games and love are two elements that do not go together, people will find love. Truth, Love, and all other Virtues will never exist within the game because they these ideas transcend game completely. The game is only useful to distinguish the real from the fake.

Last Night

Intoxicated by your Ciroc in that bottle shaped figure

I imagine what would happen if I pulled this trigger

Holding this gun only to save you, I have counteracted its use

Not to be used or abused by Cupid, just hoping that I will do it

BANG!

What Women Really Want

Women don't want a nice guy or a bow tie

They want a smart-ass with a good lie

Women want to be treated respectfully

They forget they have to respect themselves

They want emotional stimulation

They want deep conversation

But they can't be alone 'cuz these thoughts wont conjure

Afraid to ponder their lives without a man they jump helplessly like a frog to a lily pad

They look for what they don't want

So they find what they don't need

Blind faith won't take you where you want to be

And if you paid attention you wouldn't be bitter

They want Love in all the wrong places but grow afraid of making the necessary changes

They want to cuddle with a no huddle quarterback, get sacked, and run the same play

They even only want men sometimes for the thrill of the chase

They don't want too nice, or too mean

They want just right

So maybe thats why their down for the team

They want the dream seller type who makes them feel like Mrs. Right

They want to be sexy on the outer to make up for their mishaps on the inner

And wonder why at their best friend's wedding there sitting there

Still Bitter

Expectations

Many Girls have low expectations

Contrary to popular belief the bar is a mere self-construct

A set up that has no winner because what you expect isn't always what you get

Although not asking for much their dream guy is already an animation

AS SEEN ON TV

All they need then is a pipe dream that these CEO's aren't selling

Swag isn't confidence and Money doesn't mean prominence

Just a malnutrition of things not fit for a Queen

And there is nothing wrong with a dream as long as you have the patience to see it through

No matter how you feel these things do come true

That's not to say all girls are prepared for what they ask for

They want a pick of the litter, laid back, honest, booty call jigga figure 'cuz they want to be just like Beyoncé

Marvin's Room Anticipation with the same low expectations

We must not be afraid of change even when we see it happening right in front of our faces

Taking places of everything we should have been

Afraid to move in the direction opposite of them

Love is a leap of faith that sometimes will have you falling splat on your face

But it is the choices that we make that outweigh the expectations

Never- Death to Keisha Cole Poems

Don't ever say I was never there for you

Or that I never cared for you

But something happened and now you're just rappin'

Your Keisha Cole syndrome defected into your poems

I'm tired of you spilling your heart out about your ingrown relationships

Your old feelings resurrected into the next and still blaming me for your stress

I gave you my best but you decided that all of me wasn't enough

Our unity was disbanded because we were both caught red-handed

Cheating happened before we even got together

Victims of a relationship conquered without friendship

So now were broken up

Maybe we've both had enough?

Time to forgive and move on

Find new people

Life keeps going

But u don't have to write hundreds of poems about how I did you wrong.

That's not strong

Write a Poem

I'm going to write a poem for you until our 1 becomes a dividend of 2

Until you realize that I don't want u for your tries, but the real inside

It moves me to places of Love only God should be

I will travel back through time to write in your Notebook

I just hope you write back

I Want To Say

I would rather say this because my spoken
word could use some practice

But the fact is

I am still looking

That Erykah Badu type whose essence is
energetic

That soul type who's not afraid of
expression

The regression of your type makes me bite
my lips

Afraid to quit

Your hips are just as sweet as your lips

But I haven't met you yet

So all I have is the regrets that I don't even
believe in

Your spirituality is dependent of the lamb

Your mentality isn't dependent of a man

Your Jill Scott thicks are as sweet as honey dips

Guided by wisdom only fit for a queen

With the outlook of a revolutionary at the core of your being

Emotions of a poet with a flow a spoken word can live in

I want real that Brown Sugar kind of Real

Where people can watch like a movie and feel everything I feel

There's nothing that compares so every game you win

Perfect 10, and that doesn't include your physical features

Your beauty transcends the teacher and the student

Stuck in your rabbit hole, I will decide to stay in the true motherland

Love will guide us, and find us searching
for it at the same time

Meanwhile we'll hide from the lies,
inceptively asking

Why comply

So we answer through a simple try

Our reciprocation makes time fly by

'Cuz everyone knows that's when you're
having fun

Meanwhile I think you're the One

But in the midst of this entire pun

I just realized

I haven't met you yet

100 Ways

I just fell in love with your words spoken like a token to my dreams I am a fiend to your heaven

Like your favorite number is 7 symbolizing the Days it took God to create something so beautiful in nature

And I want to read your mind to see the liberator in your spirits intertwined between the lines your nurture has written

Dipped ever so gently onto that pillow creating a softer you

The blue skies have nothing on your brown eyes, and whenever I look into them I know where the truth lies

Everything about you just feels right on this sunset sighting, but the glare from your lighting is unbelievable

So I contemplate the 100 ways to your Soul, and this is the only way possible I know

What I Won't Do

I'm not going talk about girl stuff with you

I'm not going to watch your soaps just to
see your artificial Blue

I'm not going gently rub you all the right
ways until you say I Do

And I'm not going talk about my emotions
just to understand you

I will not sit here and make promises that I
won't hurt you

I won't, I won't, and I refuse to play the
chase after me games you play with all
these other dudes

Your goodies will not be a chess filled with
Gold

And I will not listen to everything I am told

I will not rub your feet just because

And I won't metaphorically drink your
bath water out of Love

Our relationship will not be perfect or a fairytale Dream

So take this as it seems

What I will do is accept the perfection of your imperfections showing me the Real is in you

Part 4: Perspective

TRUTH

Truth has many definitions and comes from many different perspectives in life. It may be hard for us to analyze or determine the truth because it can be intertwined and manipulated so easily into fallacy. Buried in the fabric of the world are a number of people that can offer truth on different matters. These individuals have master keys to the door hidden in all of us. The problem is that on the surface of the world is a bias that hides truth. We attach lies or personal interpretation to a truth like a virus that spreads every time the idea is brought to attention. The nature of a virus is to attach itself to one host, and take over as many hosts around it as it can.

The infected idea becomes so prevalent that it spreads between cultures and becomes truth for the masses. The virus continues to spread because it has a defense mechanism that allows it to defend itself. The person receiving the fallacy is affected by a lie and has also formed a viral personal defense mechanism that may work the same way creating a culture of fallacy.

Truth is in all mankind. It protects us from the lies that the media, and any other source of fallacy we encounter. It is essential to filter in the truth, and unmask the lies. We feel that everything that is not connected to personal perspective is a lie, and ultimately close ourselves off from any other truth. This lack of perspective can cause your own brain to turn on itself when a change in thought arises, and causes self-harm mentally. It is crucial to balance yourself in truth by being capable of adding other truths needed to reach enlightenment and liberation of the mind.

I am talking about strength to fight for what is right, and virtuous. I am talking about a liberated individual free from all the lies that paralyzes the mind, and keeps the body strong. I am talking about Anarchy. I am talking about those single mothers who work 3 jobs to feed their children every day. I am talking about the soldiers that fight for this country. I am talking about that father who raises his son to be a Man. I am talking about Harriet Tubman, Sojourner Truth, Frederick Douglass, Martin Luther, Martin Luther King Jr., Malcolm X, Huey Newton, Buddha, Hunter Thompson, Tupac Shakur, Winston Churchill, Cornel West, and any other man or woman that stands for what is right.

Truth cannot be fabricated nor skewed in meaning, but can be misinterpreted. Truth is infinite and has no boundaries on the people that it can change or effect. The true beings of wisdom use death only as a reminder of existence, and not a means to fear life within itself. It is up to the people to become more enlightened, and protect our social leaders that are so crucial to the people trapped in a mindset of greed, violence, and acceptance of the social norms. Change will come, but whether it is for the better is up to the people to decide.

Paperclip

Your brain supersedes your wisdom if you think it is logical to see that your pink backpack means that you have become the daughter or son of death

What you wear does not define who you are and the scar is that the par has superseded that wisdom to disdain from logic

Setting apart knowledge from power your tower's top floor is right next to the entrance door of your brains 10-story building

You are wielding from the enlightenment that enlightens you based solely on the fact that it is not in you to tell the truth

Revolution of the sub
standard proceed away from the substandard that holds your dirty little secrets

There is no cure for this cancer unless the doctor is willing to spread the antivirus to the answers

Fear will resolute in you to prove your theory of cognitive dissonance, which really means that you are in between wisdom and a hard place

Understanding comes only from the mind so what's behind the lies doesn't provide a good enough Why

People LIE, Lie, and lie just to ask why you feel so docile in your own eyes

Possibilities

Is it possible to need and want at the same time?

Subliminal to ones' mind it wonders

She says "is it possible to live life without actually living"?

 Afraid to fall under everyone else we digress with positive steps

He says "I'll do anything for the American Dream"

Depending on the content and size of the plate selling your souls seems worth it

She says, "I have to do what I have to do"

Stunted by our own decisions we envision we must get out our circumstances

Equipped with no defense we dance with the devil

Afraid of the consequences we inch in these situations hitting one joint at a time just to ease our minds

Finally were high off life hoping and praying that were doing it right

Living the dream

We bet our lives on a lifestyle

Consumed by the lies all for a small look at its pie

Death is synonymous to life

Philosophy synonymous to why

We try to simply make it taking one day at a time even if we're faking

Waking in the possibilities of a Dreamer

The way out of the World

It's hard to walk through this life without redemption

The temptation of God's will lost in translation

So you have mothers killing babies

Mothers sexing ladies

And grown men turning their 12 year old daughter to a woman

This world is fucked up

Full of tough love as if Gods love has hidden itself

A mere atom bombed into a sea of sin, and passed down

We have terrorized the blue skies not even realizing that the rainbows don't even show anymore

Not realizing that the innocence of a child don't grow no more

Free willed into believing they're grown at the age of 15

Unable to live their dreams

Victims of the stupid decisions

All because their parents never paved the way to God

So the cycle turns into an accepted ass normal facade

Not realizing that the choice will always be, and has always been yours

Stuck In Lies

Being stuck is the only buck we accept

Chasing big dreams leased out for souls is
the goal

The mis-education of our black childhood

Dilated in the ink of real nigga mindset

Living within a book called stereotypes

Not afraid to do it right just don't know
how to

The slavery can be outgrew so we cope
with the dope

Just as long as we don't become dependent
of the ignorance

Our body will never experience withdrawal

Unless your 6 foot tall your life cannot
persist of a basketball

So you become a rapper just to master the
art of selling out your own soul with shit
you wouldn't touch with a ten-foot pole

You can tell a real artist from a fake from the content of the plate

Real artist eat nothing but truth, proof with the courage to get more

Real rappers sell their plate for 50% lower than market value and a dirty whore just 'cuz it seemed like a score

The mis-education of the child left behind enemy lines

But it sounds so good these are the figures we see in the lime

Light up the blue skies with the words Dreams and Lies

A record deal isn't making it, only faking it

The true greatness comes from the people who see the road leading to enlightenment, freedom, justice, and righteousness

And taking IT

Conformity

Society as a whole is full of conformity, because people are afraid to be themselves, or people are afraid of something that they do not know. I never realized how conformed people are to culture until I realized that they protect and perpetuate a system that continuously lies, cheats, and steals. Life is not easy obviously, but the reason for that could be the fact that the emotions we have are always under attack by some external power from our societal hierarchy. Many cultures have conformed to stereotypes, racism, classism segregation, and discrimination. People conform so much that they accept it, and feel anyone trying to change it is illogical.

Forgetting

I can tell you everything you want to hear
like your life will go on without that fear of
tears

But I will tell you the truth and say that it's
up to you

Caught within the confinement of your
own time you have become subliminally
blind to the rhyme

"Only hope I had was selling dope"

Choked by these lyrics, we conjure up the
spirits of our dark future

Teaching us how to change the positions
like the Kama Sutra

But lacking the essence of the true presence
Black History gave to us

And that brave queen who would not get
off of the bus

We are forgetting

Wiped out we are not remembering the individuals who cared enough just to put the weight of the world on their back

Just so you can make it back to Black

Strong enough we lack the courage to embrace anything worth it

Ignorant to our own Courage

We surrender ourselves, and the word nigga is our white flag packed deep down in the inner city

So what will put us on the right track?

NEVER FORGET THAT YOU WERE BORN BLACK

Truth

Anyone can find truth, but the hard part is finding the premise

The blemish within your thought obtains only knowledge you have to be taught

A benefit of the doubt type thinking where someone can interpret everything they see without blinking

You will miss your train if your brain is late

Holding on the cosmic secrets

Promised sandy beaches

Meanwhile, the truth reaches way beyond the fingertips of amazing

Raisin in the Sun type living

No one will ever understand because truth is a representative of a world unseen

To enter you must replace the things that you want with what you need

Perception

It seems I am misconstrued to the rule that says you have to be commercial to be great

Or the one that says you're a man when your girl is late

'Cuz the true period between being great and not making it is a line thinner than the crack that rose grew out of

I was misconstrued to the rule that when I pick my queen she doesn't have to be a lady

Or the one that says that I have to be shady just to make ends meet to put a pair of Jordan's' on my feet.

There is no plea for my freedom from the slave master

I was misconstrued when they told me that my history didn't matter

To sit down, shut up and get fatter 'cuz the matter at hand isn't worth debating

Until I learned Lincoln was just faking

While America takes all the glory for its great military but won't take the blame for the military cemetery

It seems like a fairytale for the victims of the bourbon until that drunken hangover set in and their grenade had them wasted off pain

But I have realized the true question

Why!!!!!!

Why try to be something I'm not or don't even want to be

Why make others happy if my freedom is first to go in the plea

At the end of the day with all questions asked I look toward my past for answers and live each day like it's my last

Life

The road best traveled is one traveled alone
because truth isn't easily found in this city

Not the place for anything if you really
choose to stand for something

And when you're standing –tall better be
your motto to follow in this cold world

Right after your brain turns into a prism
full of dark figures just a pigment of your
subconscious

Unless you see the light in this darkened
place full of the colonial history we call
logic

Designed to equal a message only powerful
as your faith allows it to be

You can see a tree on fire if you're seeing
the right thing so live life for what's right
and it will turn into the right life on the
right night

Nigga

Nigger and Nigga is one of the most controversial words known to man. It is a word that changes in context when used by different cultures, but it has not changed idea. "Nigger" is a word that is so offensive that it will get a man killed, and "Nigga" is a word of great endearment. Nigga/er is a word that derives from the bias of the people that enslaved Blacks more than 300 years ago. For the past 50 years, it has been used as a slap in the face of the oppressor by the oppressed, but the "n" word is no more than a word that has evolved into a mindset or philosophy. The "n" word will never belong to any certain race because it is no more than a word. The survival of the word proves that discrimination has become more of a stereotypical perspective than a physical burden whose roots are still evident in our psyche.

Hope

For those that can't deal with the stress of life sometimes because it's overbearing

It tears the heart apart sending your insides into a mode of panic, and frantic

Creating this gigantic hole

Something so strong indeed that it has already taken over your mind plenty of times

But you overcome

And it's not for yourself, but for those people around you that push your goals

Hope leads to things unseen

Reasons to live for a teen

The secret about Hope is that it only exist when you make up in your mind that you want it to

That's when it becomes a pipe dream for fools, open for interpretation

But you don't know the evils that
you're facing

No one will look through the darkness with
a flashlight bigger than your own unless
they're in the tunnel too

But that would imply that they're walking
in your shoes

So create your own destiny, and find
wisdom for yourself

Because life offers choices you can easily
regret

Life is What You Make It and Be Who you
want to be

Because once you're oppressed mentally it's
hard to break free

Look

When you look into Darkness what do you see

Is there a deeper meaning or a light not seen

Because literally it's a black page but metaphorically it can be anything

It could be a white page taken over by darkness

But as you look closely you can see the light shine through

Now that you have noticed the light it seems like it has grew

2 times bigger than before

So that metaphor is now a reality

But in reality the ones who let their light shine through are told to keep it down because you are blinding too many people

Look closer

The more you look the farther your boring reality hits you

Don't over analyze the darkness they will tell you

But it's seeing past just the darkness that will make you a light to the darkness

So technically it's a metaphor open for interpretation once the surface has proven deeper than its appearance

Part 5: Friends

Friendship

Today, I thought about all my friends. I had not realized that all my friends are so far away from me. I started to think about the virtues that constitute friendship, and then I realized that friends have to be destined. There is a supernatural element to the connection that we have with our friends. These people come into our lives years at a time and have such a significant impact on the way we live. A real friend is hard to come by, but when we find one it is a humbling experience. A friend is somebody that is there for us through the ups and downs, trustworthy, honest, and loyal. A friend can be mistaken for a backstabber making it difficult to decipher a true friend. Friendship takes time, effort, and consistency as means of solidarity. Consistency may be my biggest factor with friendship because I hate people that are always unsure about whether or not they want to be your friend that day, month, and even year. Friendship is a skill lacking in society today because most people are so egocentric that friendship is impossible to them. So, if you have friends you should cherish them. It is too easy to come across a fake friend, and too hard to find a true friend. Life does not care if it makes us leave them behind.

Old friend

We never realize what we had until it has left

Afraid we may miss out on the best

Our friends are worth all the fights

And the times when things aren't going right

These feelings of necessary reciprocation we must fight

Sometimes even our tongue we must bite

Our friends are worth it

Gifts from God even

And trusting the lord is in this season

So look at yourself and ask what's the reason

Why that friend left

Impact

They walk into your life and then they leave

But in between they show you who you really are

Make you think you're above the bar

Not afraid to walk on water because you won't drown

Unknowingly teaching you to be you while you discover

You are so caught up on them being there that you forget at any moment they can leave

Like meaning to what you see

Making life decisions trusting that we have it right

I say we because your essence intertwines within mine

Proof that God Exist because his Love has to feel something like this

 Open minded to hold no boundaries

We travel back to the matrix that you as the guide found me

I'm only talking about Gods Law of recognition and place

Saying I see your passions so I know I've belonged forgetting to trace

Those steps only take me back and ignorance has a tax

Your brain for that change

Your love for the game

But those lies don't live here anymore

Trapped behind that closed door is your impact

You leave the road so wait for me up there after the tracks

Just Looking

I'm just looking, but I don't see the connection

That weird look that keeps you questioning

"Why are they looking at me like that?

Afraid to even look back

Your silent thoughts suggest that there is emptiness

Handed a glass container full of the sands of time told to empty it

I don't even see you anymore 'cuz the dark cloud that shrouds your being covers your soul

The gold that was once in my eye and dull ceases to shine

You are invisible because you choose not to see yourself and afraid of anyone's' help

In the end you suffer because you spent all your time looking

My Friend

You are as amazing as my perception
allows you to be

Overwhelmed by the idea that every time
you are reborn you come back stronger

You are a true friend blind of the judgment
that hates me

Blinded by fate your ambition pushes the
world past itself

Sitting still impossible to rest your
friendship is a true attest to the goodness of
God

I know I don't see you as much as I should
so I guess I'm writing this poem to show
you I'm good!!!!!

Part 6: Passion

What Are You Seeking?

Have you genuinely sat down and thought about what you truly want out of your life? What are your goals? Who do want to become? Most importantly, how will you make it there? Have you even thought about the reasons we have been given life in the first place? I have been reading this story *"The Noticer"* by Andy Andrews, and it is an extraordinary self-help book that uses many principles that will allow a person the means to reach their goals. The book makes me think about what I am going to do with my life. Am I meant to write books? Am I meant to play sports? Where am I going?

Although I do not know exactly, I do know that I have been searching for wisdom and enlightenment ever since I started writing. I have found comfort in something that can influence lives if I am skilled enough. I write as merely a humble servant to the people lost in translation to this game of Russian roulette. I realize now that we are given certain tools or gifts to find a path. We are given dreams, ambitions, and even pain in life to bless others. We are all equipped with the tools we need to succeed. I would have to say my passion is seeking wisdom in those around me and within myself. My passion is writing to enlighten others with the same experiences. My passion is freedom, and I find paradox of joy and fear within that freedom.

Tattoo My Name in History

Black Pride has been tatted on my back since birth

Free from cages enabled to see myself for who I really am

So I know it's real

I am not a nigga, but a black man

Not coexisting with my inner Man Tan

This isn't a menstrual show with Black Face

I am not here for your entertainment

I won't be the nigga I am supposed to be begging to be accepted by people that don't know me

I hate B.E.T, and loathe Tyler Perry for that reason

Same issues, different seasons and I'll tell you what kind of black man is in this very being

I will talk like I've read a book before, and be smart

I will support black intellectuals that speak from the heart

Cornel West

I will strive for greatness because the black pride before me has showed me how to be Great

I will make my father proud of me

I will say the things I'm not allowed to see

I will seek therapy from things other than weed

So Black Pride lives within

Not like every self-proclaimed nigga you see with it tatted on their forehead saying, "look at me"

Hanging from the tree saying

I know I's free but the nigga in me don't allows me to think

Please do's it for me

My father always told me that they could
never take my knowledge

So I owed it to him to go to college

Make him proud instead of dropping out

My daddy wasn't a nigga and neither was
his daddy so that word don't run in this
bloodline

This poem is to tell my grandfather in
Heaven I am doing fine

I'll carry mine

Just wish he were here to help me carry
time

Feelings

Feelings of numbness cloud my mind

Filled with Motrin I take my opinion in a
pill each morning

Mourning of a man unheard

Defined by every word but no one hears me

Fears uncontrolled to non-existence

I want my fear to define my ambition

No money or cars

Only bars that spit not out of my heart

So if I end I know were the numbness starts

Passion

My Passion grows with the woes my heart beat encounters

No matter the situation metamorphosis is delivered

But death will come regardless of my fears

I don't worry

They say a life unexamined isn't a life worth living

And what they say will play over and over in the mind of a thinker

To let up of the beliefs that you are grown into is suicide

Inevitable death to the soul

And as time passes the disrespect of wisdom reduces it flow leaving the young adult in you unable to grow

Your base is decayed so the only way to survive is to stand behind enemy lines and pretend to be brave

You are not paving the way for the next

You are only making the quicksand steeper because u were afraid to dig deeper

Looking for the words of the preacher, but the word of God lies inside you

But the lies that prove should be inside of you aren't because you have neglected your own moral responsibility to collect

And then you wonder why your soul is unable to correct its wrongs

Every lie that was ever guided to me didn't past the Why that pushed those beliefs

So to live as a conscious being means to be no one but who I continue to consciously grow to be

Standing here saying I am Free

Assumptions

I wake up with thoughts of revolt

I was taught to question everything handed
down to me

Taught to intervene that money and life
means as a passageway to my dreams

Defined by the same words and
perspectives that I live

I am assumed to be close to nothing for the
skin color I give on an application

My words are my source of felony
appeared to be imprisoned

Not supposed to be this critical thinker

Judged by many but feared by none. Quick
to shoot words but won't pick up a gun

Because stepping out on faith to share my
faith is the next topic on without a trace

Disappeared before I even figured where it
came from

Never met Uncle Tom

The word nigga is a white man's past and a black man's future with a cut so deep that u may need a suture

But u won't accept that black doctor because a black doctor is a whack doctor who couldn't have actually learned anything

Notice how I am not talking of an actual wound but a hole that resides in the black cultures soul

Our rhythm and blues has turned to a bruise only seen when we choose

I feel as though I am not supposed to be who I am

Trained for failure but destined for greatness.

I am the product of a judgment and assumption

Poetry

I was asked one day who was my favorite poet

I thought about all the greats, but as of late I have no answer

I love spoken word so much that its entity alone is my favorite

Like an archangel it delivers my prayers to the higher

The essence of these spoken words is enough to turn nouns to verbs

The poets are merely the messengers assigned from the divine

A question with no space to write the answer

Answering the question wouldn't be an answer but a guess

But even to guess of who is the best justifies nothing

Part 7: Metamorphosis and the Changing Identity

Self -Actualization

What happens when a person realizes true identity and becomes enlightened? What happens when someone discovers their true talent and begins to figure out the world? I wonder if we will we ever notice the people who realize their own boundaries that have been imposed and see the chain on our own doors. Awareness is the first stepping-stone to unlocking your full potential. After self-actualization, the enlightening experience offers a perspective that ordinary people could not possibly understand. The problem is that people that have reached this standard of self-actualization are not accepted because society fears they have become crazy.

Will we ever wonder why the morally unjust serves as power figures? In this day and age there are smart people that fear psychosis, and there are stupid people that are too ignorant to accept anything but bliss. There are hipsters, anarchist, radicals, and liberals who transcend the boundaries while close-minded conservatives sit back on their ideologies and propaganda. There is a shortage of known writers, philosophers, or people in the media that offer a conscious perspective on life. People are afraid of crossing the edge of their own boxes. Through writing, I have found that I am more of a liberal than conservative, but in my search for truth I have realized that both are vices. There is a golden mean of coexistence that allows us all to be crazy and sane at the same time.

Unknown!

Taylor is a beauty stuck between her dreams and a hard place

It seems that she is lost to the common mind because her common grind is her work

Afraid of that little door stored away next to her fairytales she had when she was a little girl

The common lie is that she won't walk through supported by the common guys she talks to

And the moment she starts to walk through, she stops to talk to the Devil

Ponders to wander the possibilities that the door within herself that is given by God is not there

She stares, as her heart grows fonder to the idea that she wanders seamlessly in the land of dreams

Without following her dreams to further support her own self

The inner self is there like she's in her closet but knows not what to wear

The important thing is that she's looking for her makeup to make up

She's fallen behind because every time she runs the sound of a gun cocks towards her Aquiles Heel

Afraid to lose her heal because she might steal Gods Heart Away

Just by Dreaming

Even dreaming to dream

That the one thing holding her back is herself

Afraid to walk through the little door that leads to Life, Love, and Happiness

The Inner Me

I am talking about the freedom to liberate

The shortcoming of justice

The cup half empty

The metaphor or the simile creating
sentences of empathy

Master of humility

Sitting 6 years under a tree of life to find
knowledge

The same knowledge spread through
homage to names like

King who delivered the dream

Thompson wrote about the fear and
loathing

Badu who maintained the two words Black
Queen

Shakur who showed what it really was to
be black outside the serene

Mandela who showed what forgiveness
really means

West who thinks of what it all really means

And all others who gave us positive things

To dream and believe

That I truly have the power to change this
utopia for the ignorant

I Wish

I wish Tupac were still changing the world
alive to guide these little girls and boys

I wish people knew every lyric to KRS One

I wish that Hunter S Thompson never
picked up that gun to cock

Take his own life 'cuz mine was
intertwined into his

I wish we really understood Kings Dreams
to his means

PEACE is spelled backwards in this society
while self- hate reigns supreme in all beings

Wishing and dreaming is where reality
starts so it's important that we all make our
mark

In someone or something's start

Greatness

Greatness is in everyone, but only a chosen few are ever blessed to find it. Greatness is a long and difficult road full of sacrifice that many have traveled and fell short or made it to the end. Many have chosen to ignore the path to greatness, and have just given up on life. Greatness is a choice. The qualities that define greatness depend on the person and the greatness sought to acquire. Ali was the king of the world. Jordan was the Air. Hunter S Thompson was Gonzo.

Tupac was the Rose that grew out of concrete. The list goes on and on, but every person I listed played a crucial role in the lives of others as living proof that hard work plus a gift can lead to greatness. Through them, we learn that people who start off typical acquire greatness. They use their area of expertise as a vehicle to reach the people. Acquiring greatness comes from practical acts of heroism bringing victory, life, and love to people depending on the circumstance. Greatness will never reveal itself because the humble nature of a Great person will overcome those feelings. We have to learn to live simply, and attempt to change ourselves. I will attain greatness, and when I do I will not run from its responsibilities.

Letter to Greatness

I know my greatness is one choice away so
I will not behave

Conform to the rules set by my Bourne
identity, torn between a rock and a hard
place

I will not fear my potential because it
defines the abilities of my future

It's the difference between assassination
and becoming more

And to tell you the truth I'd rather be
assassinated because I brought change

Don't believe in fate without choice, but
know my choices will ultimately lead me to
heavens' gate

So I will wait contently, not afraid of what's
to come

And when greatness finds me, I won't run

What About Me?

What about Me

A generation lost in translation to a nation of self- hatred

To the youngins' as we are called who realized the Dream that Martin Luther King fought for

The American legacy our forefather taught me lingers in a self-conscious I just can't seem to get rid of

Believe it or Not I'm not comfortable in this casing not meant for embracing

I feel like I'm a drug stuck in a capsule waiting to hit the acids of the stomach of death.

Living by the rules they say designed by God, but I know it's the ref

See the problem are inside of this well-spoken well rounded young man you see before you

You would get lost in my world

Caught so deep that you would betray your own conscious just to escape

I am a black man in America,

Harder to do than surviving without water, and the only way around it is to sellout my people

NO

 I won't do it, because you can't prove that the grass is greener on the other side where the prize is white with the bluest of eyes.

So what I have done is taken King, Luther, Thompson, Guevara, and anyone else worth learning from and devised my own conclusion, as you never taught me to do

So What About the Positive of my Generation as the only place we are left to go is off into the sunset unnoticed

'Cuz it seems the only thing they see in me is drugs, lies, cries violence, death

That's the same thing that ref wants the older generation to see in me so what am fighting for above

What do you do when you know you don't connect with your own people because they have taught you anything smarter than right is white?

What are you left with?

Where Are You?

Who Are You?

Do You Even Exist?

The Answers can't be described until you truly have opened your eyes that getting out the social stigma is the true prize and the fear of truth we have inside is actually a compromise.

A collection of lies designed to keep you society's boy in an orange jumpsuit on a chain gang made just for the nigga

'Cuz they're still calling my people that, but they just use the politically correct form of the word: BLACK

Only we can use a word like that which gives our people a false hope that were actually making it in America

"We got Obama"

Who can you expect a person to be when all he sees is the pain in his mother's eyes because she's working two jobs all the time

Barely Surviving

But see I was blessed

1 of the 2 black children raised by both parents where my dad stayed at home because he retired

Uncle Sam taught him well so he taught me how to maneuver through the fire

But still all society sees is another black nigga within a shell casing destined for a murder case

Truly I am weird,

Defined by myself

No fear

I AM LIVING, and I AM FREE

So What about Me?

Harrison Bergeron

My poetry is a gift

Love turned itself into it

Written so beautifully I compare the words
of the greatest poets to be a separate entity

It encompasses its own name and its own
brain

They won't amount to anything because of
a corrupt American Dream that was pie
never actually offered to eat

Only a promise that the slave owner
doesn't have to keep

It will forever stay in the darkness
underneath our eyes, all the pain that Willie
Lynch has caused me.

His theory broke the unity, but never broke
the faith of the people

Which really means that me is actually we.

So what are we silent for?

Why have u bitten your tongue so hard that
it bleeds with ignorance

Are you afraid to face the truth, or just
afraid to admit that you're not living it

Change is Gonna Come

I want to change the world

I know in order to do it I must go through it

Ignorance comes easy to those that accept their living

Complacent in nature but the philosophy lacks in literary abundance

Fear consumes the costume even when the real shows

And I have a dream were made famous by a King who wasn't scared of his oppressor

So I have a dream the Newton's law can be broken

Every action has a reaction equal in power

Every cause has a cause except for the uncaused cause so we must have the ability to change on our own

Some things are within and some are without like the dope boy mentality of the south

The same place where they started the slave trade route is the same place they trade bricks

You aint shit if you don't know what a Kilo is but the mentality is all they see so that's all they will ever be

Even the ones who can make it out don't have hope so they just sit back and choke off their infrequent living

The black community has been reduced to mere rubble and the projects prove it

Unable to be built back up because:

 1. They would rather go in debt for a bank buck

2. These white CEO'S won't hire us

3. We don't realize that these banks are trying to make money because they expect you not to know that dummy.

All part of a plan for the rich to get richer and the poor too not even exist

So when change does come try not to look so stupid

The End

In the end

I will stop

I will thank him for the trials and
tribulations

All the waiting and debating will be worth
it

I will have reached my regrets point of no
return

Defined by my Love and Hate

Virtue will prevail

Epilogue

3 Metamorphic Stages

I am grateful for first and foremost God because he has blessed me with everything I need. I am grateful to my parents for taking care of me, and teaching me. I am thankful for my sister, and brother for being there for me. I am grateful for all of my friends. I am grateful for childhood friends, and new friends. I am thankful for my home Prince Georges County, MD. I am thankful for my history, because I know where I came from which makes it easier to know where I am going. I am grateful for ideas, baseball, writing, music, and each and every artist who has left their mark on each subculture. I have realized that I can only find consistency in myself. People will come and go. Love will come and go.

I feed off the consistency of knowing that people will be there when I fall may it be school, work, and anything else that changes within society. I have been so subject to change that my adaptability is mistaken for intelligence, and my fear of commitment is growing. I use to enable the lack of consistency that drives me, but I realize I am touring to greatness, and the city is changing, but the bus is still the same. I am caught in a moral dilemma between my own stability and Anarchy. I will never have my life in perfect alignment, and I am probably just dreaming if I am. I will never choose blissful ignorance over the decision to change the world. I will never fear my own potential.

END

Acknowledgements

Lastly, I want to dedicate this book to my late grandfather Reuben Lee Adams who gives me the courage to deal with life. I want to thank my parents for supporting me. I want to thank Ms. Elizabeth Anderson who influenced me as well to begin writing, and pursue my goals.

-Jeremy M Adams